Cynical Maxims and Marginalia

Cynical Maxims and Marginalia

William Ferraiolo

iUniverse, Inc.
New York Lincoln Shanghai

Cynical Maxims and Marginalia

Copyright © 2007 by William Ferraiolo

iUniverse books may be ordered through booksellers or by contacting:

iUniverse
2021 Pine Lake Road, Suite 100
Lincoln, NE 68512
www.iuniverse.com
1-800-Authors (1-800-288-4677)

ISBN: 978-0-595-45092-3 (pbk)
ISBN: 978-0-595-89403-1 (ebk)

Printed in the United States of America

For those who do not quite fit in—and for R

Contents

Preface

Professional philosophers in the Western tradition are trained to present and explain their arguments and defend their theories in painstaking, even excruciating detail. This practice is indispensable to academic disputation and analysis, but it can also be tedious and tiresome—especially for the reader. Occasionally, even a reasonably cautious philosopher gets the urge to cut loose and let a few blazing rhetorical arrows fly without all the additional background explanation and supporting sub-argument. Feeling that my quiver of arrows has remained untouched for too long, I decided to compile a loosely associated collection of maxims, aphorisms, apothegms, provocative questions and other shots in the dark. The compilation has been great fun to produce, and has served as a kind of vacation from the rigors of closely controlled academic analysis and adjudication. I hope to say more, imply more, and provoke more, with a pithy arsenal of carefully chosen phrases than is typically accomplished in the usual philosopher's treatise. I am not, of course, the first disaffected crank to attempt such a departure from philosophy's traditional methodology and, thankfully, several useful models have been graciously provided by some of the genre's most accomplished curmudgeons.

One especially shining example is worthy of particular mention. In 1665, François duc de La Rochefoucauld, published his *Maxims*—a slim volume of piercingly cynical and brutally penetrating reflections on the all-too-human condition. As something of an armchair cynic and (at least) part-time misanthrope myself, I am forever in the Frenchman's debt. Seldom has mankind and its pretensions received such a richly deserved drubbing in print. His book remains a work of bitingly beautiful genius. Loosely following the master's example, I have attempted, once again, to hold our vanity and many other peccadilloes up to the bright light of criticism, skeptical dissection, and well warranted ridicule. I do so, however, in full recognition that I hold the mirror up to myself, and my own various and sundry failings, along with the rest of the sometimes painfully human race. I claim to be neither holier nor wiser than any "thou". We are all inmates in one sprawling asylum.

Over three centuries have elapsed since the first publication of La Rochefoucauld's *Maxims* subjected us all to disconcerting scrutiny and public mockery—much to the delight of the day's smug intelligentsia. That, I say, is long enough. If imitation is a form of flattery, then I hope that this collection of maxims, one-liners, rhetorical questions, and loosely associated musings, makes me at least something of a flatter, even if I do not quite rise to Rouchefoucauldian heights of misanthropic artistry. At the very least, I hope to revivify the fading tradition of aphoristic meditations concerning the various absurdities that constitute the human enterprise. It is worthwhile to periodically expose the self-aggrandizement, pettiness, and irrationality that saturate our nasty, brutish, short, and (at least) slightly silly lives. It is also an entertaining pastime.

These reflections are intended to be full of pith, punch, and at least an occasional insight regarding our common foibles and delusions. Like the *Maxims* by which it is loosely inspired, this work is *not* intended as a comprehensive effort at psychoanalysis, a robust existential exploration, or an example of minutely controlled philosophical argumentation. Much is, quite intentionally, left unsaid. As in so many other areas of endeavor, I am particularly proud of the work that I have *not* done. I have resisted the temptation to attempt to say that which cannot or should not be said. When it comes to that which *cannot* be said, what choice did I really have? I have also left out much of that which *should* not be said because it would detract from the effect of playfully suggested possibilities left to be interpreted from the reader's unique perspective. The reader has a contribution to make to this work, and I mean not to deprive anyone of an opportunity to contribute. I have also declined to indulge in great lengths of tedious explanation, exegesis, and critical evaluation. As a professional philosopher, I already have to do more than enough of that when I am working at my real job (if one can call philosophy a "real job"). Just as poetry must omit the bulk of background and detail in order that it remain poetry, so too must this collection of stray thoughts leave much to the reader's imagination if it is to remain what I intended it to be. Sometimes, an idea must be left on its own to provoke, edify, offend, or fall completely flat. My hope is that each numbered item in my *Cynical Maxims and Marginalia* might function as a kind of cognitive projectile, and that at least some of them might pierce the reader's pretensions, illusions, and unexamined assumptions, providing a jolt, a flash of insight, or at least a good laugh at mankind's expense. There is little effort here to prove any point, demonstrate any claim, or justify any supposition. Persuasion is of secondary interest. The first intention is to incite, to puncture, and to awaken the reader from slumber. The maxim is my weapon of choice—my scattershot delivery system. I let fly in all directions, but I take particular aim at no one—or at everyone (which amounts to much the same thing). This is not exactly a work of traditional philosophy, but it is a not-too-distant relation—somewhat more playful, though pointed, and a little haphazard. Philosophy can (take it from someone who does it for a living) turn out a bit dull, dry, and pedantic. There is often a kind of interminable precision about it. Careful conceptual analysis has its place and value, but so does firing off a quiver full of lit and burning arrows. Here are some shots that I just had to loose into the darkness. Take cover.

Modernity and America

1. Ours is a culture of obsessive self-absorption. We are also increasingly self-destructive. This is no coincidence. We are sick and tired of ourselves.

2. We voluntarily enslave ourselves to the attitudes, beliefs, and values to which our ancestors have unreflectively adhered. We prostrate ourselves before altars built by the blind.

3. The United States is now more of a marketplace than a nation—and even in this it is failing.

4. A new "dysfunction" emerges. We may call it *tolerance deficit disorder*. The condition is characterized by a refusal to put up with more nonsense than is necessary. Those afflicted with it are our last, best hope.

5. Incompetence has become the norm in the public sphere. It is almost a treat to find someone doing a job properly.

6. What need is there to be a "friction against the machine"? Let those who wish to power the machine sacrifice themselves to it. "But," you say, "this machine will kill us all!" Well, of course it will. That is hardly a reason for histrionics. Just stand aside as the machine careens off course. Raise a glass to it if you wish.

7.   In the West, we seek to slake our many thirsts. In the East, there are still some who know how to remain still. The East has greater hope that it may endure. Of course, it is all the same either way.

8.   There is far too much talking today. Very little of what anyone says is actually worth saying—or hearing.

9.   We moderns have lost the ability to derive sustained fulfillment from feeling ourselves simply existing as part of the natural world. We demand synthetic entertainments.

10. We live in an age of perpetual adolescence. Our culture rewards those who refuse to grow up. When adolescence comes to be regarded as a virtue and adulthood a vice, societal collapse cannot be far off—or so we may, at least, hope.

11. Who has not felt like a three-legged lion dragging itself toward a herd of vaguely bemused antelope?

12. Let us retain the option of retiring from the world and enjoying solitude or the company of a like-minded band of expatriates from modernity. This is no judgment against reality as it stands, but only a recognition that other possibilities are not to be closed off simply because they are not popular among the masses.

13. Can those who are authentic be anything other than outcasts? It is pretense that unites a culture.

14. We like to believe that technology serves our interests, but many of those interests are spawned by technology itself. Do simple, nomadic peoples need all the accoutrements without which denizens of New York or Tokyo would fall to pieces?

15. Modernity offers us convenience, comfort and innumerable diversions. In exchange, we are required to accept a degree of domestication that our pre-modern ancestors would have regarded as slavery.

16. The West is all industry, but the East knows how to bide its time.

17. Small towns in the United States are the repositories of American nostalgia. The big cities are laboratories of American pathology. As for pathological nostalgia—one must have recourse to Hollywood.

18. The United States is a near-sighted colossus flailing wildly about itself—whether in joyous dance or savage rage it is impossible to tell.

19. Surely, our best citizens must be our least recognized. The real work is not for show.

20. What, in the contemporary world, is more oppressive than the ceaseless prattle and blathering? Media and mouths relentlessly bleat at us as if we have grown terrified of silence. No one can be truly civil who does not have the capacity to be in another's company without filling every moment with sound.

21. Can the modern world not simply shut up for a moment?

22. Too fast, too loud, too much, and too coarse—these are the hallmarks of modernity.

23. Far too often, the mere fact that something *can* be done is treated as sufficient cause for doing it. Perhaps there is under-

appreciated benefit in understanding which things are most in need of being left undone—and even not contemplated.

24. The human body was not intended to endure sustained stress and anxiety. Fight or flight must be options briefly entertained, not persistent characteristics of waking life.

25. Is there any element of our culture that is not in a fairly advanced stage of rot? If so, rest assured that it will be outsourced in due time. America is rapidly relinquishing the capacity to embrace anything that is not coarse and ignoble.

26. We do not even use the *word* "ignoble" any longer. There is nothing left to which such terms may draw a contrast.

27. Aristocracy is all well and good, provided a reliable means of identifying the *best* and most noble among any given population. Absent this, we seem to rely on size and ferocity as markers of excellence.

28. There are interesting people living today. One can obtain their phone numbers.

29. We rarely experience those parts of our world that have neither roads nor train tracks running through them. The most compelling landscapes are inaccessible from the perspective of the most ordinary routes of travel.

30. Nothing is more American than breakfast at a diner and semi-coherent blather concerning political issues that one does not really understand.

31. We often specify conditions under which "the terrorists win," but terrorists cannot *win*—they can only kill.

32. We may, on occasion, need to behave fiercely in order to survive. It is, however, less than obvious that those most willing to behave fiercely are also those whose survival is most salutary.

33. We live as if we are under constant scrutiny though, in fact, most of us would barely be missed if we were to disappear into thin air. Can it be that we are scrutinized precisely *because* we do not matter?

34. Anyone advocating that the whole village ought to have a hand in raising the child cannot have met too many of the villagers.

35. Cyberspace allows for the instantaneous dissemination of pathologies that once had to migrate through face-to-face contact. Now, a perversion or vice can claim victims around the globe and normalize itself from the "net roots" up.

36. There is a tipping point at which some pathology becomes sufficiently commonplace that those afflicted constitute a cultural voting bloc. When some new turpitude gains the equivalent of a political action committee, complete with lobbyists, we may be confident that it is here to stay.

37. Why do so many people speak so loudly and interrupt so frequently? It is as if they confuse conversation with combat.

38. The handshake is a vaguely simian barbarism. There are more sanitary modes of greeting that do not involve gripping and squeezing the free end of a proffered appendage.

39. A horror movie is not quite effective if the audience does not, at least once during its course, find itself rooting for dead teenagers.

40. One cannot but suspect that there is a covert, but dimly acknowledged, competition functioning with something like anti-evolutionary pressures at the societal level. It seems that the most obnoxious are now the fittest for survival. Perhaps it is a kind of justice after all.

41. At the movies, there is at least a reasonable expectation that one's companion will, at long last, shut up for a while.

42. Nurses are almost invariably cruel. Their experience of human suffering has inured them to all manner of whimpering and complaint. It is difficult to impress a nurse by brandishing one's pain.

43. The conformist endeavors to see the world as others see it and, therefore, does not see the world at all.

44. One would have thought litigation superior to dueling for the purpose of settling disputes—provided that one had not met a lawyer.

45. We do not even see what we want to see anymore—we see what we are told to see.

46. The perpetrator of the hoax carefully calibrates his respect for the public and its powers of imagination. He understands that many of us wish to be fooled, and demand fabrications to alleviate our boredom with ourselves.

47. There is something incongruous in war protesters who shriek their hatred of "the war machine" and those manipulating its controls. Are they not waging war against the "warmongers"? What kind of advocate for peace cannot behave peaceably?

48. No narcotic is so widely abused as television.

49. Dancing for any reason other than joy is both cheap and dishonest—no matter how talented a dancer one may be.

50. We are now more dependent upon pharmaceuticals than we are upon the family. Drugs are, after all, more reliable.

Politics

51. It is not possible to be overly cynical about politics and government. One might profitably compare Congress to a brothel—but this would be an unjustifiable disparagement of prostitutes.

52. Citizens are not mere tools to be used to satisfy the whims of those in government. The proper relationship is nearly the reverse. Many invite their own servitude and then bemoan it the rest of their days. Others enslave themselves to the pursuit of freedom. Rarely, someone simply steps aside to watch the show.

53. A unified world government can result in nothing other than univocal, pervasive tyranny and oppression.

54. Politics is an expedient for those minds incapable of turning inward. Our leaders are invariably those who are most estranged from themselves.

55. In a democracy, the public gets what it deserves—but remains perpetually convinced that it is being relentlessly ill-used. The same may be said generally of marriage.

56. Political power is just another form of indentured servitude. This is why all politicians are flatterers, dissemblers, and chameleons changing color at the behest of each new crowd.

There is greater power by far in disdain for political office. There is, for that matter, greater power in disdain generally than may ever be gained by persuasion.

57. Those persons for whom two major political parties suffice are the same persons for whom two basic ideas suffice. These are the binary souls. They are either very wise or very stupid.

58. Let us assume that a two party system adequately provides for a reasonable diversity of ideological opinion and modes of practical, political endeavor. Now, let us assume that hotdogs and bratwurst represent a reasonable range of the full scope of culinary and gustatory interests. On second thought, perhaps it is best to pause and reflect a bit on our assumptions.

59. There is no such thing as a propagandist without bloody hands.

60. Terror is not only the implement of the terrorist, but of the fascist as well. Theirs is an unholy symbiosis.

61. It is not possible to negotiate with those who intend one's destruction—unless, of course, one regards one's survival as negotiable. Is the matter out of the question?

62. Beware beautiful women, charismatic men, and all mention of the "common good".

63. The distinction between lobbying and bribery is much like the distinction between reindeer and caribou—it is not even a matter of semantics.

64. Compromise is mutual failure. It does not follow that there is any shame in it.

65. By government's lights, the anarchist is unreasonable. By the anarchist's lights, government is an insult.

66. Our democracy is representative in roughly the same sense that the Roman Empire was "Holy".

67. Patriotism is a sham unless a nation is truly worthy of the devotion its patriotic citizens profess. Therefore, it is always a sham.

68. The air of imperturbability is the single most effective bargaining chip.

69. We do not disagree as often as we believe that we do. Very often, the illusion of discord arises because we occupy incommensurable perspectives. What appears to be ideological conflict is, in reality, shouting in different languages for which there can be no translation.

70. Socialism is only a system for nationalizing compassion so that individuals may be done with it.

71. No citizen of a democracy will ever vote for a politician who tells the truth. This is largely because the truth is that democracy requires better citizens.

72. In a democracy, stupidity always holds the majority in every chamber of government. It is, after all, a representative system.

73. Our political system has become so corrupt that one can no longer even vote with clean hands.

74. We vote for those forms of corruption and dishonesty that we find most palatable.

75. What is a partisan but one who has announced an intention to lie, cheat, and engage in corruption for the benefit of one group as against another? If the preferred side is actually always in the right, then partisanship is not required, but only honesty and fortitude. Which group is it, by the way, that stands infallibly on the side of righteousness?

76. What is wrong with the enjoyment of bread and circuses? Of course they are merely distractions to conceal the intentions and actions of the powerful and the corrupt. Should we prefer not to be distracted? Should we be forced to watch the malfeasance unfold—or are we expected to believe that vigilant awareness might actually stem the corruption? The powerful shall always have their way (it is almost a tautology). Let us at least have a little bread—and, perhaps, some dancing elephants.

77. The common good shall be secured as soon as it is available at a take-out window.

78. The expression "talking points" is a not-too-clever euphemism for *lies that we all agree to tell together*.

79. The most glorious and most lasting phase of any empire is its collapse.

80. A certain type of man becomes indignant at the imagined injustice of being forced to tell the truth in public. This type of man is the politician.

81. We often hope that our elected officials are lying to us, because the alternative is that they really are the rank imbeciles that they appear to be. The greater concern, perhaps, is that we, the voters, really are the imbeciles that *we* appear to be. It may well

be that we inverately vote for liars and imbeciles because we insist upon a government in our image.

82. A politician under oath is a bit like a tumor under chemotherapy.

83. Imposing mandatory national service is a pathetic expedient for nations that do not inspire voluntary self-sacrifice.

84. Politicians respond to simple "yes or no" questions as vampires respond to garlic.

85. We convince ourselves that we are not susceptible to manipulation despite mountains of evidence to the contrary.

86. An honest politician appears on the scene as often as a celibate whore.

87. The term "political scandal" is, at best, a redundancy. The scandal is that we have found the need to indulge in the political at all.

Impermanence

88. Do we strive after esteem, honor, fame, or respect? What are these but the evanescence of paltry beings hurtling toward individual death and, ultimately, extinction as a species? Why is it worthwhile to be briefly revered by a race of transients that will, in the very (or, perhaps, not so very) long run, vanish from this universe without leaving so much as a trace? One may as well be Pope of Atlantis.

89. The ravages of old age are no less just than the bloom and vigor of youth.

90. There is a sense in which everything that anyone ever does is insignificant and meaningless. The ocean of time will ultimately swallow and destroy it all. Should we, therefore, do nothing? Perhaps. For many, after all, doing nothing would be something of an improvement.

91. There are neither beginnings nor ends in nature—there are only transformations.

92. One and the same life force animates each of us and all the many living things. Perhaps it is expressed in inanimate matter as well. It permeates and suffuses whatever faculties and capacities may be present in each material manifestation. Where sufficient complexity is present, the life force can see, hear, feel—and even reason—provided a brain equipped for the

task. Upon dissolution of the material form, the life force loses access to the defunct systems of cognitive function in this particular mode of the material world, but there is always more where that came from. The life force persists and animates all transformations of the stuff of life. We are ephemera through which the life force briefly expresses itself. When we are worn out, the life force tries on a new suit of clothes.

93. All of this little globe and those who reside here will, ultimately, be lost to the vastness of time and space. This is one reason that fame is properly despised. Compared to the ocean in which we swim, we are but droplets. Fame, infamy, and anonymity are equally negligible.

94. A lifetime of pain and suffering is as nothing compared with an eternity free of bodily frailty. We exaggerate our travails because we think that our bodies are ourselves. If we are just bodies, then we are trifling things indeed. What is the significance of our suffering if we are no more than haphazardly animated flesh?

95. Is it not our searching that makes us feel lost? When we look for something else, something other than that which is right here, right now, we thereby reject our current experience. If we simply embrace life as it is right now, then there is nothing for which we must search. Being lost entails wanting to be somewhere else. No one who wants to be where he is ever declares himself lost.

96. There is a flow that underwrites the phenomena of experience. The flow has no form, but form arises and dissipates within the flow. No form is permanent, no thing immutable. All is unfolding. All is *unfoldingness*—itself.

97. Evolution does not sort for contentment or satisfaction—it merely provides incentive for reproductive efficiency. Who would expect happiness to persist much beyond the conclusion of the procreative effort? Indeed, why suppose more than the briefest and most parsimonious concomitance available?

98. All of the physical world unfolds, evolves, and flows change upon change. We tend to think that it is an array of permanent, immutable, things-in-themselves that undergo the various changes, but upon inspection, there are no things-in-themselves to be found—but only flux. We invite horrors when we try to hold flux fixed. Permanence is not the way of the world.

99. All things pass, and thus, are not *things*.

100. What is it to "make the world a better place"? Given that all life in the universe is in the process of being destroyed, "improvements" to this world must consist in staving off the realization that lives end, along with some attempt to make their relatively brief duration somewhat more palatable (or, at least, to seem so).

101. Is youth wasted on the young? It may be that the most admirable dispensation of youthful energy is creatively wasting it.

102. An entire novel is written for the sake of one or two lines. A whole life may be lived for the sake of a few moments.

103. Anxiety is both self-aggrandizement and denigration of the rich, unfolding pageant within which the alleged "self" is embedded and into which it ultimately dissolves. Anxiety is a failure to recognize the interconnectedness of all phenomena and the stability of the ultimate reality (whatever it may be).

Does it then follow that the world itself experiences the anxiety with which our paltry "selves" are plagued? Does the world tremble as we do? Should it?

104. What can be more absurd than the charge of futility, issued by the man who spends his brief life storing up material wealth? What is more futile than that?

105. Time does not *pass*—it is absorbed.

106. The future is not different in kind from the past and the present. It is only our relationship to the future that sets it apart. We foolishly believe that it does not yet exist merely because we cannot yet see it.

107. We do not exactly get older. It is more correct to say that our current experience feels more worn than before.

108. To hurry is to express contempt for the here and now. Where is the evidence that we rush toward a greater good?

109. Our representations of reality are constrained and shaped, at least in part, by the world as it is in itself. The world itself is, in no way, constrained or shaped by our representations of it. The world makes us—we do not make it.

110. Nothing is as fragile and unstable as our illusions of safety. Few things are as secure as our insistence upon maintaining such illusions.

111. Can there be fewer than infinitely many universes? Only if there is but one.

112. Time does not ravage us, but only exposes our true nature. Dissolution is the way of the world.

Reason and Its Limitations

113. The world is as it is and not as it might otherwise have been. How much needless suffering and foolishness results from our persistent failure to appreciate and accept this plain fact? Concern with "what might have been" is not merely sad, it is also irrational ingratitude in the face of what is. How foolish to denigrate the broad panoply of reality with dismissal in favor of attachment to a world that never was.

114. A thing may be rationally justified but unendurable nonetheless.

115. Anyone who gets upset about matters beyond his control is being irrational and is inviting needless suffering and distress. Virtually everyone is guilty of this form of irrationality, and this guilt is typically compounded daily. Tremendous psychological and emotional trauma could be averted if all of us declined to get upset over things that we cannot control. We know this, but it seems that we will not (or cannot) stop.

116. Complaining about the state of one's life is a bit like complaining about the amount of one's lottery winnings, or the windfall tax.

117. True wisdom is unflappable. Perturbation afflicts us only when our reason fails.

118. We do not need anger to impel us to effort and accomplishment. The wise understand that effort unencumbered by the burden of anger is more efficient and less troublesome to all concerned.

119. Quixotic endeavors are the only truly ennobling adventures. One does not become a real adult without tilting at least once at a windmill.

120. An author produces but one masterwork. The rest is marginalia.

121. We often want things that we know to be self-destructive and unhealthy. Fix that! How—by appealing to self-interest?

122. The world always wins. Contending against it is the common folly. Knowing this changes nothing.

123. No one *goes* mad. Rather, madness comes calling. Like a virus, it can sustain itself only where there is a host that offers shelter.

124. There is something oppressive about flatlands—as if nature declined to exert itself.

125. Most of us fail to embrace the world unfolding all around us—and through us. We wish it to be otherwise in many ways. It is, of course, as it is and not as it otherwise might have been. We are often distressed by the world as it stands. This is a petulant waste.

126. Sometimes a shrug is the best that anyone can do.

Stupidity and Foolishness

127. What kind of an imbecile tries to impress others by showing them the size and quality of his home or car? Moreover, what kind of imbecile is actually impressed by such things? It is a bit like reverence before a fat man and all of the food he must have eaten in attaining such girth. Should we congratulate the man who smokes the most cigarettes or shoots himself full of the highest quality narcotics? Our attitudes about the uses and misuses of wealth stand in need of revaluation. Why do we not ridicule the idiots who live in mansions?

128. How many embarrassing stupidities shall we say are the common property of the whole of humanity? All of them.

129. To make the world a better place—this is a fool's errand. Now let us give thanks for the fools.

130. Pride is not a sin so much as a stupidity. What do we accomplish, what do we become, that is anything more than events in due course as the world will have them? Do we take credit for the world? If so, then let us be prepared to assume the blame as well. Only a fool takes credit for brute fact.

131. There appears to be something akin to centrifugal force exhibited in the rational sphere. One can almost feel oneself intellectually propelled outward from an imbecile's center of gravity.

132. We bridle more vigorously when criticized by strangers than when upbraided by friends. We assume that strangers are more honest and have no particular axe to grind. This, of course, is foolish.

133. There are relatively few transgressions for which stupidity is not an adequate excuse. For this we should all give thanks.

134. Stupidity is the commonest and most degenerative of all human maladies. The victim does not even know that a cure is needed. This is all well and good, as the cure has proven elusive.

135. The imbecile does not understand that others are not quite as stupid as he.

136. Only a fool has an answer ready when asked what he wants on his tombstone. A bigger fool conjures up an answer on the spot.

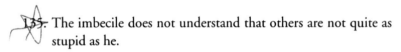

137. The family patriarch always becomes an embarrassment—at least to himself.

138. We are forever reading nonsense into the events of our lives. Our experiences are not allegories representing something *else*.

139. It is folly to believe that one will escape judgment merely because one refrains from judging others.

140. It seems that there is an inverse relationship between volume and value. Real wisdom does not require a bullhorn.

141. Silence is the most unsettling response to stupidity. A pointed silence is not apathy or acquiescence—it is irrefutable repudiation.

142. A danger does not seem quite real until we become convinced that it is too late.

Good and Evil

143. Virtuous action rewards the agent by increasing his virtue. Increased virtue disposes the agent to virtuous action. It is a virtuous cycle.

144. To expend energy upon that which does not respond to the expenditure is absurd and wasteful. It is much wiser and more felicitous to spend one's energy in self-improvement and self-discipline. One may be able to alter one's character in certain respects through sustained effort of the will. Another person's character, however, is beyond one's own reach. One may exhort, cajole, and even threaten—but one chooses, ultimately, only one's own way.

145. People who speak of moral "gray areas" do so, almost without exception, to veil their own vice from both themselves and the world. No one ever finds a "gray area" hovering about his own rights, liberties, life, or loved ones. These, of course, are sacrosanct. It is only "the other" who inhabits the "gray area".

146. A man who does not labor under the burden of guilt cannot have thought carefully about his past.

147. No one can deprive another of his decency. Each of us has the power to lay his virtue down and walk away from it. So long as we do not voluntarily relinquish it or allow it to atrophy, our decency is inalienable.

148. Only a fool attempts to make peace with those who are incapable of peaceful relations. Those who are at war with themselves can never be at peace with others. If offered an olive branch, they light it on fire.

149. Turning the other cheek betrays a deficit of imagination.

150. A man unfettered by conscience will not be forestalled by civil law. Only internal restraints have any power—external ones are merely obstacles to be circumvented. The licentious soul does not require a license, but only an opportunity.

151. Virtue is its own reward, or there is none. Vice provides only those rewards that are valued by the vicious. Those who trade away virtue for such rewards never had anything of their own to barter in the first place. Their virtue was not truly theirs, but was (unfortunately) only left in their keeping for a while.

152. Our prurient interests are no less a part of us than are our noblest yearnings.

153. The price of theft, the "karmic consequence" of the act, is that one thereby makes oneself a thief. There is no escaping this consequence. It is a necessary concomitant of theft, as being a murderer is a necessary concomitant of killing without justification. This is one sense in which karma is inescapable. We are what we do. This is why virtue is its own reward, and vice its own punishment.

154. People speak of the horrors of man's inhumanity to man as if men fall from the sky fully formed with cruel, hardened hearts and dead eyes.

155. How much suffering flows from our irrational pursuit of acceptance by those whom we neither respect nor admire? To be despised or ridiculed by the mob at large is surely no great detriment. Virtue is not determined by a show of hands.

156. Much that is obvious goes unnoticed by most of us precisely because we are so often trying to uncover that which is hidden. We assume that the hidden is of greater value and greater consequence than the obvious. We believe that the hidden is more valuable because we have to work and sacrifice to find it. Deprive us of access to the ocean of air through which we thoughtlessly plod every day, and the value of the obvious becomes instantly and painfully clear.

157. If moral rules pertain to anything at all, one can be held responsible only for those things that answer directly to the call of one's will. Beyond our decisions, desires, and attitudes, each of us is quite powerless. Praise and blame cannot be sensibly ascribed to any agent except insofar as his agency, his will, is concerned.

158. We do not blame rabid dogs for their condition, but we kill them all the same. Is it not possible to take the same attitude toward the incorrigible criminal (provided, of course, that he really is incorrigible)? Do not blame the scoundrel, for who knows the full etiology of his character and proclivities, but, by all means, prevent him from running riot across the quiet countryside. We need not assign blame merely to protect ourselves.

159. What should we have made of *Moby Dick* if Ahab had killed the whale? Would the work have lacked a moral, or might it have turned into a kind of comedy?

160. Haste makes not only for waste, but also aggression, ill will, irritability, impatience, and a generally explosive disposition. Combine these characteristics with the carelessness that attends hurry, and even a saint begins to get a taste for blood.

161. Misplaced loyalty may be unhealthy, unwise, and even deadly—but it always retains at least a hint of nobility. It is still loyalty after all.

162. What is meant by "equality"? If it is a matter of actual similarity in various capacities, then produce evidence for the alleged symmetry—as well as evidence to dispel the appearance of broad disparities in ability and understanding. If "equality" refers instead to an abstraction or a regulative principle, then it is only an attempt at emotional coercion—a bit of psycho-cultural bullying.

163. There may be no honor among thieves, but this is hardly a distinguishing characteristic.

164. The true worth of a dollar is to be calculated by reference to that which had to be sacrificed so as to obtain it.

165. How did *black* and *white* get to be the colors of a strict disjunction? What happened to *red*? The color of blood must not be dismissed from such proceedings—as it is typically not far removed from an ultimatum.

166. The patriot fails to recognize the many contingencies of birth. Would most not as avidly oppose their own side had they simply been born to parents of the "enemy"?

167. We have ceased to be shocked by any revelation. No admission is so tawdry as to raise our eyebrows. Is this because we have become more honest, or less?

168. We adopt values in precisely the same manner that we acquire scars.

169. Is it audacity that dismisses the inquiry into right and wrong, good and evil? Is it disinterest? Can we suffer from moral fatigue? Perhaps such questions are worth less than the candle. Perhaps it is wrong to say so.

170. A monster behaves monstrously. Is this an evil? Is it weakness? Is it cruelty? Perhaps, but to expect better or otherwise from a monster is at least as inexcusable. Let us be more authentic than that.

171. Do unto others, as you would have them do unto you? Let us not be presumptuous.

172. When we are aware that violence begets more violence, and continue to indulge in it, one cannot but suspect sadism, masochism, or a slothful indifference.

173. Cruelty continues to shock us though history shows us that it is at least as much the rule as the exception.

174. If the horrors of war are necessary, then how great must be the horrors that necessitate it? When bombs become the preferred mode of communication, something, somehow, has gone awry.

175. Justice demands pretense. Equality before the law is, at best, a sham.

176. Murderers are no more free agents than are hurricanes. Our revulsion is a function of the fact that we can imagine ourselves in the murderer's place, whereas we cannot see ourselves as blind, bashing forces of nature (though these are, at root, much the same thing).

177. If sloth is a sin, then nature is filled with sinners—except, of course, for the predators.

178. Publicly, we revere the peacemakers, but in our private fantasies we are all tyrants and warlords. No one entertains secret dreams of compromise.

179. Regret is dishonesty. We pretend not to remember our real motivations or the intensity of pleasures derived from our deeds.

180. We look away when we become capable of imagining ourselves subjected to the horrors that we witness.

181. Irreverence is neither virtue nor vice in the adolescent. Then again, adolescents may be invulnerable to valuation.

182. War is not a failure of diplomacy. War is a success for those who regard the world as a sprawling marketplace.

183. We love the ocean because it holds out the possibility that our sins may be washed away.

184. Being a "good citizen" is largely a matter of emulating the least interesting members of one's society.

185. We condemn others so that we have an excuse to parade our own imagined virtue.

186. Thank goodness for criminals. They make the rest of us appear so much more virtuous than we actually are.

187. Some men manage not to be corrupted by power. This is almost a shame.

188. Praise and blame are only expedients for those who cannot help themselves.

189. The most effective response to any accusation of vice or turpitude is to embrace the characterization. In this way, one almost always catches the accuser off guard and dissipates the force of the charge.

190. Where there is a total absence of respect, there can be no compassion. Those who do not respect themselves are, therefore, the most susceptible to the lure of cruelty.

191. Is the most virtuous parent the one most willing to indulge in vice if necessary to protect the children, or is it more virtuous to be principled and watch the children die?

192. The child can forgive the incompetent parent, and even the cruel one, but it is imperative that the children of such parents grow up as early as possible. This is, of course, not generally the actual way of things.

193. What does one truly believe if one professes values that do not accord with one's actions? Should observers believe their ears or their eyes?

194. A bribe holds out no temptation for anyone who values decency more than illusion.

195. We increase our freedom commensurate with the sphere of matters concerning which we are not willing to compromise our values.

196. Passing judgment on the world is as tiring as it is inefficacious—much like screaming at a mountain.

197. That which we shun delimits our field of experience.

198. Sometimes we confess because guilt drives us to do so. Sometimes we confess because it is the best way to cause further suffering. Mostly, though, we confess because we are appalled at the idea that we should have to hide our true selves in submission before the judgment of others. So, interestingly, it is pride that often drives us to confess our sins.

199. Should we work harder to conceal our flaws, to improve ourselves, or to renounce all concern for vice and virtue? Can such renunciation be itself a vice? Is it not possible to be disinterested in this question as well?

200. We reward cruelty at least as often and at least as handsomely as we reward kindness. The former is, after all, closer to the heart than the latter.

201. When in Rome, one ought to do as the Romans do, but from this it does not follow that the Romans do right in all that they do. In fact, it does not even follow that one ought to have gone to Rome.

202. Hatred is a laser projection of intense suffering. It is also reflexive. No one hates without directing hatred back, ultimately, at the point from which it emanates.

203. A writer embraced by the masses ought to hang his head in shame as he enters the bank to deposit his royalties. On the other hand, why do we never speak of the banker's shame?

204. None of us would be here were it not for the asteroid that killed the dinosaurs. The asteroid is not, for that, a great good or a great evil. It is only a great rock.

205. Nature is not subject to normative evaluation. There is no such thing as an event that *should* occur, nor are there occurrences that *ought not* to have happened. Things just collide.

206. Compassion is separated from cruelty by no more than a good night's sleep.

207. One does not deserve praise for refraining from some act that lies beyond one's capacity for mischief. Similarly, one cannot be blamed for failing to understand that which simply lies beyond one's understanding.

208. Regretting an act is not quite the same as wishing for the chance to live the moment over again. One may, after all, wish to retain the regret.

209. How much warfare might have been averted by the refusal to indulge in oversimplified labels? A nameless hatred cannot long endure.

210. There are few outrages that still go unrewarded.

211. Obscenity is profitable precisely to the degree that it meets with condemnation. Who ever wasted hard earned money on sanctioned smut?

212. Some criminals lose as much as they gain by rehabilitation.

213. The utilitarian morality of "the greatest good for the greatest number" conceives each of us as nothing more than expendable cells within the civic body.

214. Where food is scarce, decency is scarcer.

215. We are sometimes told that some ancient battle saw the slaughter of all the men and all the horses on one side. Should we not be suspicious of the alleged slaughter of the horses?

216. Rehabilitation without punishment is like birth without labor.

217. Vulgarity is not, in and of itself, a talent—though one can display talent with vulgarity as a prop.

218. Weeds are not less worthy of life than grain.

Religion

219. There either is or is not a God, a Creator, of some type. Perhaps some people know for certain which is the case. Those of us who cannot honestly count ourselves among that number should embrace the fact that we are enormously fortunate in either case. If there is a God, we are lucky that God decided to create our world and us. If there is no God, we have won the mother of all lotteries.

220. Buddhists do not bow to *each other* in greeting. They bow to that which is shared by all.

221. Every moment is every bit as real as every other moment. Any peculiarity or special character is wholly imagined by those who forget that the universe is large, and old, and takes no notice of their adventures and interests. If there is a God who notices, then all is equally miraculous.

222. Reverence costs no money, takes no time, and detracts nothing of value from one's life.

223. Do not insist upon evidence concerning matters for which evidence cannot be had. If a man says that he fears God, do not demand a demonstration.

224. What if God is not a being or an entity but is, instead, a way of the world's unfolding? Can God *occur*? Does God *happen*? Perhaps God is already over.

225. Of all the animals, only man manages anxiety about the future. This is, perhaps, the chief consequence of the Fall.

226. There are no souls, no selves—or there is one shared by all. Either way, all that arises must pass away and all of us are just passing through on our way to nowhere in particular.

227. What is "faith"? If it is believing propositions for which one lacks evidence or, worse yet, for which ample evidence to the contrary exists, then "faith" is, at best, simpleminded credulity and, at worst, poisonous perversion—the "rational animal" recalcitrant at the constraints of reason. If, however, "faith" refers to a certain attitude of optimism or an insistence upon interpreting experience in the most hopeful light available, then one cannot but boggle at the leery reticence with which so many of the "faithful" appear to regard "God's world".

228. Tibetan Buddhists make elaborate, beautiful *mandalas* of colored sand, look at them for a bit, and then sweep them away into nothingness. Has any religious ritual ever exceeded this in purity or understanding?

229. As soon as a religion develops ritual and law, it is corrupted. Ritual and law do not salve our suffering.

230. The cross is too often used as a club—or a switchblade.

231. The beginning of wisdom is in knowing what to leave alone. This is what is meant by "the fear of God".

232. The primary function of religious faith is affording the faithful a justification for denigrating the faithless. Those who believe that they have God on their side are often the most dangerous of His creatures.

233. The sincerity of religious belief is inversely proportional to the amount of time spent in selfish pursuits—or the number of one's possessions.

234. Any religion that does not teach us that we are all manifestations of one underlying life force can only be a construct conjured up by those who are alienated from this most fundamental fact of our condition.

235. We admire confidence even when it is unfounded. As proof, simply note all the works of art devoted to saints.

236. Hagiography is the last resort of the flatterer. Can we not leave the dead in their holes?

237. The Sermon on the Mount is either staggeringly noble or stunningly naïve. It is often difficult to tell these two apart.

238. The kind of certainty that leads to religious warfare is a brand of knowledge without which we might readily make do.

239. No one is more obnoxious than a man brandishing his certainty like a club with which to knock sense into the rest of us.

240. The people who insist that God is everywhere are usually the same people trying to corral us into churches, mosques, and synagogues.

241. Karma is introduced as an expedient to explain away the apparent injustice surrounding us. One wonders, of course,

why horrific suffering and hideous injustice are presumed to be merely *apparent*. Without this assumption, what remains to be explained?

242. Pilgrimage presupposes that some places possess a power, or proximity to the holy, that is inaccessible from the pilgrim's customary environs. Merchants along the route piously embrace this view.

243. Show me three reasons to hold out hope for mankind, and I will show you the Father, the Son, and the Holy Ghost.

244. The *Old Testament* offers moral teachings through the medium of mass slaughter. The *Word* is written in blood.

245. Nothing carrying a price tag can be properly regarded as sacred. Of course, it does not follow that the sacred is necessarily priceless—or the profane without its charms and value.

246. The Buddha wanted nothing to do with blind faith, and he did not demand obeisance to some unseen divinity. For these reasons, he is the noblest of "spiritualists".

247. The heretic depends upon the Inquisition for his identity.

248. Our culture has no tradition of begging bowls, but only of panhandling for change. There is an aesthetic difference. The offer and acceptance of food is, somehow, a matter of greater intimacy than an exchange of funds.

249. Of course a beggar may be a chooser. Men have, after all, chosen starvation.

250. Freedom is always freedom *from* some constraint or compulsion. More than this is not offered to mortals. Perhaps God is

free in a deeper sense, but mankind lives in a world of causal law and we are subsumed thereby. Be content then to be determined by the dictates of reason and not the wild impulses of the passions. This is as "free" as one is permitted to be.

251. Those who deploy the word of God for manipulative purposes violate the commandment prohibiting covetousness—not to mention the injunction against false witness.

252. If God made man in His image, let us abandon any hope for the afterlife.

253. If Noah had refused to build the ark, he might have prevented the flood. What good, after all, is a deluge that leaves *everyone* in watery graves? Religion requires survivors as chastisement of the dead.

254. Perhaps we have gone forth and multiplied enough.

255. The gods of Olympus had the last laugh. They disappeared and left us to our own devices.

Brutal Truth

256. Honesty is not fundamentally a matter of *telling* the truth; it is a state of character disposed toward *accepting* the truth whatever it may be.

257. Very few people actually want to know the truth—though they pretend to revere it. Most only want to know a handful of particularly comforting truths with which to salve themselves or through which they may claim vindication.

258. There is less than a cat's whisker separating the cynic and the realist.

259. Has anyone ever actually been made happier, in more than fleeting fashion, by the acquisition of a large sum of money? Clearly, there are those who *pretend* to have attained happiness in this way. Can this be more than pretense?

260. The human condition is not *susceptible* to absurdity—it *is* an absurdity.

261. Most people are more interested in appearing to know things than in actually understanding anything—the poverty of appearances, for example.

262. Most apologies are insincere, and all are motivated by self-interest.

263. All "tolerance" is pretense and sham. We do not need to tolerate that which we love. That which we hate we *ipso facto* find intolerable. What we neither love nor hate, we do not tolerate, but simply observe—or ignore.

264. There are few forms of relief that outstrip a long overdue bowel movement.

265. Compassion is pretense far more often than it is sincere. Either that, or cynicism has gained far more sway than it deserves.

266. Subtlety is a form of cowardice. Many know this, but most are too subtle to say so.

267. It may be true that we are all equal insofar as our apparent differences are merely illusory. Is it not, however, true that some illusions are preferable to others? If not, then why blather on about equality for the edification of illusory others?

268. Dogs are honest. Dogs beg and exhibit no shame. Cats lie. They are barely able to conceal their contempt.

269. It is rare that one truly meets another person. Typically, we are introduced to a façade, a caricature of the real person underneath it all, behind the show. What we meet up with is an attempt to manifest a character for public consumption. The public persona is so far removed from the primitive, pre-conditioned person that the two are, in the best case, like distant relatives—more than once removed.

270. What a pity that so much remains unthinkable, and that so much thought remains unsaid (because unendurable). One cannot help but wonder how much of value has remained unexpressed for fear of public disapprobation and ostracism. A

kind of intellectual and putatively "moral" squeamishness inhibits the kind of honesty that is required for living an authentic, full-blooded life. The truth need not be comforting, "fair," or easily digested. Sometimes the truth, especially about our genuine nature, our real interests, and our honest motivations, is a terrifying or even bestial business. It is not, for that, any the less true than our more palatable aspects.

271. What a shame it is that so many of us have never received a proper beating.

272. Let the truth be spoken even if it breaks us apart. If we are so fragile and brittle as to disintegrate at the expression of hard facts, then it is best to be done with the farce and have ourselves shattered once and for all. If the truth is too much for us, then we are too little for the truth.

273. Some celebrities, if we are to be honest, do well to die young. How sad would have been the spectacle of a shriveled Marilyn Monroe or a decrepit and enfeebled Elvis Presley. Given the general brevity of human life, the handful of years they "lost" are best not mourned for the missing.

274. The marketplace does not reward honesty.

275. Is it, in fact, "A tale told by an idiot"? Is it correct to describe it as, "Sound and fury signifying nothing"? Really ... this overestimates the case. Shakespeare was an optimist. For this he is to be forgiven.

276. To admire an adversary is to recognize a bit of one's own incompleteness. One may see the value even in that which one seeks to destroy.

277. We convince ourselves to hold out hope because it is easier than accepting the truth.

278. An honest pessimist makes no attempt to persuade anyone that life is, in fact, as he perceives it. Any hope of success would be grounds for optimism.

279. Most conversation is simply a matter of passing time until we find an excuse to be done with each other.

280. A friend is someone who pretends to be more deeply affected by our travails than is actually the case.

281. One who seeks unconditional love is best advised to get a dog—and feed it well.

282. Pain teaches us lessons that we are otherwise unwilling to learn. Those who fail to learn even from their own suffering are the most incompetent and forlorn among us.

283. Most of us prefer to know the truth about others while demanding that others accept fictions about ourselves.

284. A conversation without food or drink is tolerable only to the oppressed.

285. The Earth does not need us to "save" it. The Earth does not, in fact, *need* us at all.

286. The appeal to tradition betrays a lack of self-confidence, imagination, and integrity.

287. The parent's desire of a better life for the children generally extends only as far as the material realm. Parents want their children to be better *off* than themselves—not *better*.

288. To know something and to acknowledge it—these are two entirely separate conditions.

289. We see others neither as they are nor as we are. Both the other and oneself exist only as embedded moments within the seeing.

290. Any friendship that is endangered by a squabble over money could not have been anything more than business in the first place.

291. Can it be that the next plague will improve the world?

292. The misanthrope is the only one who truly believes that we are all created equal.

293. Self-destructiveness is just narcissism mixed with misanthropy.

294. No other species is nearly so disappointed in itself as mankind.

295. Only the inveterate hypocrite still takes hypocrisy seriously.

296. The wise are never offended or insulted—but their bones are no harder to break than anyone else's.

297. Hope remained in Pandora's box after the other contents had escaped. Most do not understand that this is the greatest tragedy of the affair.

298. It has become all but impossible to so much as broach the subject of race without being labeled a racist. There is no one for whom this constitutes a greater tragedy than those who have been victims of racism.

299. Is it possible that one can lack the strength for a justifiable sui-
cide? Can one be better off dead, but too squeamish or
deluded to do what is necessary? In such a case, one's life is
one's punishment.

300. An expression does not become meaningful simply because it
is uttered with a grave countenance or hissed through gritted
teeth.

301. Why can we not, once and for all, admit that we do not want
the truth? We may *need* it, we may see (on occasion) its value,
but we do not love it more than we love our illusions. Our illusions have, after all, been with us much longer.

302. There is no such thing as gratuitous violence. It is all equally
necessary.

303. Why is a meaningful life preferable to, for example, a comfortable chair? The latter, it seems, provides greater ease at lesser
cost—yet we write no odes to the comfortable chair.

304. If we all derived pleasure from pain, torturers would be held
up as saints.

305. Is gratitude incompatible with bemusement? Let us hope not,
because honesty demands both from us as we consider our
place in the world. Perhaps it is honesty that makes for an
uneasy dissonance in the assessment of our circumstances. If
so, a solution presents itself.

306. How often does the toast, "To your health!" thinly veil a curse?

307. Why do we pretend, in public, to be happier than we really
are? Is dissatisfaction really so humiliating? Would we be more

forthright about our discontent if others were more forthcoming about theirs?

308. Repentance before an audience cannot be trusted. Private repentance, on the other hand, cannot be common property. We cannot, therefore, trust that another man truly repents.

309. Unsolicited advice is like an attempted circumcision.

310. Who among us does not occasionally revel in a stereotype? We can be honest when we are "among our own". We must speak the truth about ourselves, at least to each other—provided that the truth does not touch the parts that we hide even from "our own".

311. If a man puts a gun to your head and makes demands of you, the only way to deprive him of his power is to dare him to pull the trigger.

312. To whom does the asylum not occasionally beckon?

313. It is easy to spot the optimists in intensive care—their charts are marked "Do not resuscitate."

314. The greatest humanitarians refrain from explaining themselves. They also know how to mask their true feelings.

315. We cannot all be honest any more than we can all be taller than average. Let us not demand more from the general run of humanity than its fragility may bear. It is, frankly, a wonder that we ever find sufficient cause to tell the truth at all.

316. It is most disconcerting that conspiracies no longer require clandestine skullduggery. They now occur in the bright light

of day. We are even encouraged to buy shares in them, as they are traded in high volume on the New York Stock Exchange.

317. The average man decides what he *wants* to believe, and then derides any and all evidence to the contrary.

318. It is often those who refuse to accept help that remain most inveterately in need. From this it does not, of course, follow that the destitute are necessarily the most stubborn or willful of our fellow beings. Many who would accept assistance with utmost gratitude manage, nonetheless, to break our hearts.

319. Sometimes one can offer nothing beyond a general disinclination.

320. Hand a man an excuse, and he is sure to make the most of it.

321. Some say that there are no ghosts. One wonders if they have not met their neighbors.

322. If you find an honest man, leave him be. It is the only hope for either of you.

323. Those who express disdain for mankind have always been the most interesting among us.

324. The term "population density" does not only refer to the number of residents per square mile. There are other senses in which a population may be properly described as "dense".

325. When we are not principled in our opposition, we thereby lend support to our adversary.

326. It is a tortured soul that insists upon believing only the truth about itself.

327. It is an unfortunate man who has not had occasion to taste his own blood.

328. The con artist sees us for what we truly are. The master con artist understands that he is one of us.

329. Putative concern for the welfare of "the children" is the most pervasive form of hucksterism.

Men and Women

330. Men need women much more than women need men (generally speaking, of course). A woman without a man may go childless, but a man without a woman will degenerate into a sickly, grasping creature filled with malevolence, self-loathing, and hopelessness. Exceptions exist, and good for them, but are they to be admired? The question is sincere.

331. Men like guns because they are not especially fond of conversation.

332. Few things are as sad as the spectacle of a woman who has been convinced that strength and independence require her to behave as if she were a man.

333. Raising a child without the father is a great misfortune. Doing so intentionally, unforced, is indefensible.

334. If men and women truly understood each other, would their mutual affection be enhanced, or would it disappear altogether? We shall, of course, never know.

335. Carnal relations are wildly overrated and, also, quite remarkably exciting, intense and pleasurable. Sex is fantastic—but not all that it is cracked up to be.

336. No one who pays any attention to the math would even contemplate having children. No one who fails to pay attention to the math is quite prepared to contemplate having children.

337. I decline to reproduce. There is more than enough of me already.

338. That physical beauty often encases stupidity is no great surprise. The shock is that awareness of the illusion so seldom insulates against prestidigitation. Why does the conjurer's flourish still hold us rapt even after we know the trick? Perhaps, when all is said and done, we really prefer to be taken in.

339. Only a saint can be sincerely patient with an unattractive woman.

340. Any author attempting to explain his work indulges in a perversion. What would we think of a prostitute who felt compelled to demonstrate that she could lie on her back?

341. Would it still have been a tragedy if Oedipus had killed Jocasta as well? Might there not have been a kind of vindication in that—at least for the audience? There would, after all, have been a bit less psychobabble had she not abandoned the boy.

342. Love exposes the most vulnerable and most hidden parts of us. This is why we cling so desperately to our beloved when she seeks to slip away.

343. Beauty is a snare in which we are less than reluctant to be caught.

344. Whoever said that what we do not know does not hurt us never experienced doubt as to his lover's fidelity.

345. When a love affair has run its course, the script always seems to end long before the final curtain.

346. To say that two perspectives are *incommensurable* is to assert that, although they share the same object, or that they "look out" on the same *thing-in-itself*, there is, nonetheless, no means of translating the one worldview into a form that can be properly understood from the standpoint of the other. Mutual understanding is simply not an option. From this, it should be clear that each of us occupies a perspective that is incommensurable with all the others. Let us then dispense with all talk of "understanding" each other. This possibility is excluded by our very natures.

347. A man's physical peak is almost invariably devoted to self-destruction.

348. In reality, the woman both gives and receives the marriage proposal. The man is necessary only insofar as a ventriloquist act requires a dummy.

349. We anticipate far too much when we hope for happiness from one another.

350. A perceptive man can tell, within the first few seconds of a phone conversation, that the woman on the other end of the line is naked. An adept woman knows how to sound nude even if she wears a scarf and winter coat.

351. One demands far too much of marriage because of the ready availability of divorce.

352. Most men are more comfortable issuing public insults than they are offering private apologies.

353. Do not try to appeal to the object of your affection. Instead, work on improving yourself, so that your beloved may have a worthy companion if your admiration is one day returned.

354. A woman who really wants to flee a man's company does not back away smiling politely.

355. A woman's laughter is tinged with cruelty far more often than she would have the rest of us believe.

356. An insidious hoax was perpetrated when sexual intercourse was first referred to as "making love". Love is best expressed in other venues—those not quite so saturated with the chemicals of copulation.

357. Love at first sight is no excuse for marriage—but, then again, what is?

358. Men seek the dangerous places because they are frightened of lives devoid of danger.

359. The ones that we want are often the ones that are already taken. Would we still want them otherwise? Oh, how much fun it would be to find out.

360. There is something of the vampire in many relationships—a kind of mutual (and mutually deleterious), feeding.

361. Some women are exceptionally gifted in the arts of walking, sitting, and standing. Others are more concerned with utility than artistry in such matters. One suspects that they suffer from a somewhat anemic sense of "utility".

362. Inscrutability is a double-edged sword. The mystery may or may not seem worth the effort.

363. Love and death are the great levelers. No man in either condition can remain on his high horse.

364. It is painful to listen to a man attempting to provide a rational justification for his love of a woman. There are cases in which any rationale corrupts the thing itself.

365. A prostitute's shame is not that she takes money for sex, but rather that she *admits* it.

366. A husband does not truly appreciate his wife if he does not occasionally demand something indecent of her. No woman (outside of the nunnery) wishes to be locked into a state of perpetual purity.

367. Beauty is an inherently relational phenomenon. The concept of "intrinsic beauty" is no more sensible than the concept of "intrinsic diplomacy".

368. The most beautiful women are seldom the most gifted in the carnal arts—yet, somehow, men seem to prefer the eye's delight even where pleasures of the flesh ought to take the lead.

Mind and Language

369. The expression "the mind" does not refer to anything at all. When one uses the word "mind," one does not speak of any entity or process—physical, non-physical, or otherwise. Trying to discover the nature of "the mind" is every bit as wrong-headed a project as is trying to paint a picture of the difference between two objects—not of the objects themselves, but of "the difference" as if that were a separable entity.

370. Dissatisfaction is ingratitude. It is also weakness.

371. If you cannot will the means, then you cannot will the end. You can *want* it, but you cannot *will* it. Wanting things that you cannot will is a sure recipe for frustration. Learn then to want only those things that you can will, and you will never find yourself wanting.

372. Happiness must ensue—it must not be one's aim.

373. Only consciousness moves. All else simply is—past, present, and future stand perfectly still.

374. Dreams are congeries of the dreamer's mind, and everything in dreams unfolds as manifestations of one consciousness. All characters, scenery, and events, are projections and creations emanating from one underlying dreamer. The dream is insubstantial in and of itself; it depends upon the dreamer for its

form and evolution. Might not the same be said for all our waking experience as well?

375. The dreamer does not die, but only awakens. Characters in dreams do not die when the dreamer awakens, but their insubstantiality is revealed in what Indian philosophy calls *sublation*. I am either dreamer or I am dreamed. What then is there to fear?

376. Once I dreamed that I had awakened—only to find that my awakening was part of the dream. This I discovered upon awakening. What shall I discover upon the next awakening?

377. If we concerned ourselves as often with the workings of our own minds as we do those of others, our troubles would be reduced to almost nothing.

378. There seems to be space between thoughts (or perhaps *time* between). Is it possible to remain in touch with that space?

379. Do not forget that we consume with our eyes and ears as well as our mouths.

380. The quiet mind may be the greatest of all palliatives, purgatives, and tonics. To let the world spin while remaining still at its center, and knowing that stillness deeply, is the healthiest thing that one can do.

381. Words are largely inadequate for characterizing reality and our experiences. Much of what we encounter lies beyond the reach of descriptions or explanations. What words cannot touch, we must leave to the dispensations of that which does not rely on words.

382. Imagine your fondest dream come true. Now imagine your fondest dream dashed. Have you done anything different in imagining the former as opposed to the latter? How far removed are the two eventualities really?

383. So often, we feel lost precisely because we insist upon trying to find our way.

384. Not all thinking is localized within the brain. For some types of conceptualization, the body is an ineliminable instrument. It is not only a limited brain that precludes a flounder conceiving a waltz.

385. We love to be entertained because we do not love our own minds.

386. From where do we gain our confidence in the future? Can it be found anywhere other than our experience with the past? We believe in continuity because we have no alternative.

387. Walking is the healthiest form of exercise for the mind.

388. We do not think thoughts any more than we breathe breaths or sneeze sneezes. The breathing and the sneezing simply occur of their own accord. Attempts to prevent either are bound for failure and/or injury. It is the same with thinking.

389. The mind is its own plaything.

390. Many people are far too promiscuous with the contents of their minds. Allowing random others an intellectual intimacy with oneself invites both contempt and contamination.

391. We may get to know the territory when we travel on foot, but we will certainly become much better acquainted with ourselves.

392. It is irrational to blame a man for anything that his brain makes him do. None of us is in a position to lord it over our brains. We are no more than ministers to the ruling grey matter.

393. We could not long endure each other if we could all read minds.

394. It is not possible to distinguish between a night of wild-eyed desperation and an evening of heartfelt revelry.

395. Blessed are the forgetful, for they shall be delivered from themselves.

396. We think in short, relatively disorganized, and often discordant bursts. In the cognitive arena, most of us are semi-competent pointillists struggling against a canvas that will not hold still.

397. The mind is easily thrown into disarray. Even a glance or a whisper can send it tumbling.

398. Those who do not govern their thoughts have no hope of governing their actions. Sometimes the doing *is* the thinking. They are not always two separate acts.

399. Artists refuse to leave the ineffable unsaid.

400. A man who never entertains inconsistent thoughts and never has occasion to contradict some previous claim that he has

made, can only be an accountant—and not a particularly interesting one at that.

401. We prefer fictions narrated in a voice reminiscent of our own—but not too much so.

402. The world is denigrated by those in the grip of delusion concerning the alleged grandeur of the unseen.

403. Language distorts and conceals at least as much of the world as it elucidates.

Education and "Intellectuals"

404. The proliferation of colleges and universities, a consequence of the dramatic increase in the number of people who erroneously believe themselves competent students, has been disastrous to the quality of higher education.

405. The true academic has no desire that facts should turn out thus or so. Such desires are solely for salesmen.

406. We provide higher education to the masses in much the same way that one might provide a ladder to a jellyfish.

407. Miscommunication among "intellectuals" is at least as much the rule as the exception. Were it not so, many academic journals would cease to exist—not to mention many academics.

408. Intellectual honesty is among the rarest characteristics of the "intellectual". Most academics will dedicate a full career to denying, evading, and obfuscating an error rather than publicly admitting that they have been wrong. An ocean of duplicity must be siphoned from the professional journals so that we may identify a few worthwhile loci of exploration.

409. Many "intellectuals" are, at heart, bullies who lack the brawn to grab men by their shirt collars. Instead, they grip where they believe that they may best lay hold.

410. The wish to be understood is a manifestation of insecurity—and no one is more insecure than the "intellectual".

411. Those who seek to corrupt us always claim that they intend to edify.

412. To call a book a "classic" is simply to note a persistent prejudice.

413. A novel does not really begin on its first page. The reader's entire life serves as prologue and backdrop for the tale.

414. When we truly have no idea what it is that drives and motivates us, when we have given up any hope of ever understanding ourselves, or those we love, then we set about concocting theories.

415. Forgetting the right things is an indispensable element of a proper education.

416. No one can accomplish anything by doing nothing. That, of course, has not discouraged the attempt.

417. The most crucial lessons cannot be taught but must, nonetheless, be learned.

418. What professors teach, they have learned from some book or other. One cannot help but wonder then what exactly is the need of the professor?

419. Most students pursue their education in much the same way that men in myths chase down rainbows. They seek the pot of gold at the end, but remain oblivious of the intrinsic beauty to be found in the thing itself.

420. Maxims are for the small and the inadequate. In other words, they are for us all.

421. Do we live "lives of quiet desperation"? Well, it seems that some are not so quiet as they might be.

422. Show me the man who has not been misunderstood, and I will show you the man who has had nothing to say—much, no doubt, to his credit.

423. Nothing is truly learned that is not learned for its own sake.

424. Academics often express themselves in language calculated to conceal the fact that they simply are not saying anything.

Self

425. We all wonder what happened to the selves that we remember from childhood. We forget that, as children, we loved to play hide and seek. Our former selves do not hide *from* us—they hide *as* us.

426. The vast majority of all human effort is misdirected. We labor away at the external world when but a few internal adjustments would suffice for embracing life as it stands. We burn ourselves up in pursuit of our desires when we could much more readily and profitably lay down the desire and have done with the chase.

427. The self-destructive impulse is nearly as powerful as the impulse to self-preservation. It manifests in behaviors universally known to be corrosive to body, mind, character, and family. Such behaviors are so common as to establish a claim to a species-wide pandemic.

428. The breath can be held *outside* the body also. Do we breathe breaths, or does the breath breathe us?

429. When things do not turn out as you wish, the problem is the wishing.

430. The world always wins. The wise do not contend against it. Instead, they find their place in the flow of things and are carried along in the current.

431. Our lives are mutually incommensurable. It simply is not possible to experience reality as another person experiences it. Even if it were possible to live so much as one moment as someone else, that would be a moment forever lost from the annals of oneself.

432. We are either eternal beings or we are nothing (or, perhaps, nothing more than change itself). What is this "I" we speak of, if we are just physical processes proceeding from fertilization to dissolution? Am "I" just a stream of events? Is *that* nothing? Events themselves may be of interest, but where am "I" to be found in a sequence of "slices" through space and time?

433. Most people have no idea who they are. This is not surprising. After all, how much time do most of us spend curled up with ourselves?

434. The only real failure is inadequate self-discipline.

435. Drugs and alcohol are so popular because most people are horrified at the thought of being confronted by themselves unadorned and unmediated. Who does not recoil before a mirror unsuspected? Does the mirror recoil as well?

436. Imagine a moment of perfect contentment. Now stop. What is the difference? Become the difference.

437. The least trustworthy witness to a man's character is that man himself. We neither see ourselves as we are, nor do we speak

the truth about what we see. The worst way to get to know a man is to ask him about himself.

438. Give a man everything he has ever wanted and, in fairly short order, he will turn his windfall into implements of self-destruction.

439. The greatest stories cannot be told. One can, at best, point out a path along which a traveler might hope to find himself absorbed in some corner of the unfolding tale.

440. The self is the illusion over which we stumble.

441. Self-examination can become an unhealthy fetish. There is a kind of narcissism at the root of excessive introspection. None of us is quite so interesting.

442. We often seek to change ourselves when simply accepting ourselves as we are would obviate any need for change. A miserable failure may be unable to prevent his being a failure, but his misery is largely his own doing. Perhaps we cannot help but fail, but it is not at all clear that we must hate ourselves for it.

443. Show me the benefit in self-loathing and I will join you in it. Until such proof may be proffered, however, forgive me if I leave you to your torment and private *auto-da-fé*.

444. Solitude and loneliness are indistinguishable to the observer. Nothing tangible, nothing open to empirical investigation separates them. For the subject, however, they stand as far apart as the hosts of Heaven and the vaults of Hell.

445. We drink because we have not been taught to sit alone with ourselves and be content. This should not be taken as an indictment of the drunkard.

446. There is no such thing as escaping reality. There is only a retreat into one of its narrow and lonely corridors.

447. We are never so much ourselves as when we have been compelled for too long to be among others.

448. Why would anyone expect language to be adequate to the task of explaining ourselves? Even a mirror fails to show the back of the head.

449. In the final analysis, there cannot be more than one of us—though there may be not even this many.

450. The greatest writers do not tell stories or entertain their readers. The greatest writers compel their readers to set about self-improvement. They make their readers demand more of themselves.

451. The greatest moments of virtuosity are entirely devoid of effort. Truly great performances occur without agency or agent. Where the self appears, greatness is excluded.

452. In his final moments, did Caesar feel himself to be a man, a king, a god—or can it be that in "Et tu, Brute," he declared his realization that his assassin was himself?

453. It is a mistake to believe that the love of money is the root of all evil—it is only a branch. The root is the love of *self*.

454. Those who have not attended to their breath and noted the peculiar rhythms of its passing in and out of themselves cannot

quite embrace the immediacy of the present moment. They are out of step with themselves.

455. We cobble together a sense of self out of stories we are told by others. The truth or falsity of such stories is beside the point. Fact or fiction, they only need to penetrate and wind up enclosed by our flesh.

Simplicity

456. Wealth is a relation between one's desires and one's holdings. Dissatisfaction with our holdings is poverty—no matter how much we hold (imagining, foolishly, that it is really ours to keep).

457. Our possessions belong to us solely in a legal sense. But the world takes no notice of our paltry laws, and we do not truly possess anything that remains in the world after we have made our exit. We merely get to use a few trinkets, our bodies included, until we can hold them no longer. So many live their lives as if they get to keep things. Do they not see what the dead have left behind?

458. All that has not been entrusted to me must, therefore, be left to some other (or to no one). So, I am a fool if I allow myself to be troubled by it—like a dog barking as the caravan moves on.

459. If all of your problems could be solved with a sufficient quantity of money, then your life is impoverished indeed. Money only solves problems stemming from a lack of money.

460. Watch a dog at leisure and see what it is to be at one with the world. Watch a dog when his master returns home and see what it is to experience undiluted joy. Few people can match a dog in either simplicity or sincerity.

461. Dogs do not become bored—they sleep. This reveals the wisdom of simplicity. When there is nothing to be done, rest and gather strength.

462. Never run from a dog. It makes the dog want to chase and bite. Do not offer a dog the temptation of pursuit. Do not behave like prey.

463. A man who has no warm spot in his heart for a puppy is the same sort of man who does not butter a dinner roll.

464. Animals are content precisely to the degree that they lack imagination.

465. Alexander sliced through the Gordian Knot in one stroke because he knew better than to be overawed by complexity.

466. The simple life allows us to be ourselves. Complexity requires us to construct personae to which we are, in fact, barely related.

467. Voluntary poverty is noble. Involuntary poverty is no less so than unearned wealth.

468. He who possesses nothing cannot fall victim to the sneak thief.

469. The contrarian is every bit as unimaginative as the conformist—but, somehow, not quite as contemptible. Conformists live longer, but not so that anyone would really notice.

470. To possess a great deal is to ensure great loss.

471. Buddha, Jesus, Socrates, and Gandhi possessed almost nothing, and advised others likewise. Are we, who possess so much,

wiser or better than they? Perhaps the very fact that we possess so much indicates the answer.

472. Posterity, if we allow it the possibility of coming to be, will regard our consumption as we regard burnings at the stake.

473. Almost any object dropped into the toilet becomes unnecessary.

474. To agree that wealth does not increase virtue, and to yet spend all our time and energy in desperate acquisition, consumption, and ostentatious displays of wealth—can there be any clearer sign of our contempt for our own decency?

475. One talent is enough. We need not be virtuosos in every field of human endeavor. No talent is plenty—provided that one does not insist upon any.

476. Needless complexity is an assault on our native condition.

477. It may be better to rule in Hell than to serve in Heaven, but is it not better still to neither rule nor serve here on Earth? The life devoid of obligation has much to recommend it.

478. Why must one apologize for being no one in particular? To whom do we owe this obligation to "make something of ourselves"?

479. Simplicity has become a mode of non-conformism because so many of us have become so revoltingly "sophisticated". We are afflicted by subtlety as by a virus.

480. It is only in stillness that we find the humanity in us. In activity, we are all beasts of prey.

481. When we want to demonstrate reverence, we move slowly. There is a kind of cavalier dismissal in haste. Only in slowness is it possible to express any depth of feeling.

482. Each of our possessions is a link in the chains that we fashion for ourselves.

483. Only if we are prepared to give away our most cherished possessions do we stand any chance of deriving real enjoyment from them.

484. The creative use of space is more important than the wise deployment of objects.

485. Almost any meal eaten in good company is palatable enough, and no food is so delectable as to overcome distasteful companions at the table.

486. Do not lend money—give it away and, thereafter, allow yourself no further concern with it. Any amount too great be given away is also too great to be loaned.

487. There can be neither grace nor peace without the love of simple things.

488. Do not request an explanation of why *three* is more than *two*. Not everything is susceptible to explanation in terms of simpler facts.

Forgiveness

489. Forgiveness is wiser and healthier than indignation and rage. Anger is seductive and like any seductress, may lead us into temptations from which there is no recovery.

490. What if we are all the same being after all? Would we really be gentler toward one another?

491. Forgiveness is not for the benefit of the transgressor or the sinner. Genuine forgiveness derives from the impulse to cleanse oneself.

492. Trust is always tinged with hope.

493. Trust in another is always confidence in oneself. One trusts one's judgment of the other's character. This is the real reason that a broken trust cuts so deeply.

494. When we truly understand, are we more likely to forgive, or to recoil in horror?

495. It is not especially unfair to dislike a man due to the sound of his voice. It is about as good a reason as any.

496. The root of forgiveness is always self-interest. Ultimately, one forgives oneself—or no one at all.

497. We more easily forgive a great episodic evil than a small habitual annoyance. The former may be a mistake, but the latter is in the blood.

498. Forgiveness must be unconditional. Otherwise, it is a form of bartering. One cannot both forgive and demand restitution at the same time.

499. It is possible to become the kind of man at whom even a mime shouts curses.

500. We cherish the illusion of freedom, but freedom itself is beyond us. Though we may be unconstrained and uncompelled by those forces and entities of which we are aware, it is never possible to be free of those compulsions arising from heredity and the subtleties of our environment's impingements upon our genetic endowment. The world fashions us and we are as we must be. It is easier to forgive when we understand that none of us, ultimately, authors himself.

Vanity

501. Beauty becomes disfigurement if it refuses to acknowledge old age.

502. We pretend to know much more than we actually do know. No one knows why we do this—though many pretend that they do.

503. Why the acute dread of failure? Surely, we all realize, at some level, that even our most humiliating moments change nothing about the world. Our insignificance precludes truly eventful failure—like a worm that cannot dig. Our failures count for even less than our successes.

504. A pawn is not subject to checkmate.

505. Parenthood is the greatest conceit. The attempt to reproduce oneself, or a reasonable facsimile, betrays arrogance unparalleled by any work of art, science, or politics. The world is to be improved by the increase and dissemination of the materials of the self—the more of *me*, the better.

506. All of us carry the mark of Cain. It is the fragile ego.

507. No one ever earned entrance into the world, and no one ever earned any contingencies of birth. The initial conditions of our existence are entirely beyond our doing—yet, at some

point, we begin to take credit for our successes. This is like a slave claiming credit for being sold to a wealthy man with a large estate.

508. Humiliation effectively inoculates against vanity.

509. Most people travel solely for the sake of being able to claim that they have done so—while pretending desperately to have been enriched and edified by their journeys. Without the promise of an audience, the tourist trade would shrivel like a raisin in the sun.

510. Were it not for the desperation to impress one another, our economy, our academies, and our artistry would fall almost immediately to ruin. This would not, on balance, be a misfortune.

511. Is it possible that the most enviable life is that which goes most thoroughly unnoticed by the masses? Let anonymity be held up as a cardinal virtue, and let us refrain from praising those who most richly deserve our honor. Be no one, and be content.

512. Nothing is so chilling as a real challenge to our most basic assumptions and our most fundamental values. It is as if the life that one has thus far lived were to be judged a sham. This possibility is, by the way, a proposition worth considering.

513. The expression, "There, but for the grace of God, go I" is comprehensible only as a manifestation of acute self-absorption. Compassion that extends only as far as one's own potential misfortune is nothing more than vanity dressed in rags.

514. We are all heroes of stories that do not deserve even to be heard, much less written.

515. Most of us are of no account. Our abilities are less than impressive, and our accomplishments are meager at best. This is as it should be. There is no shame in an insignificant life. There is only shame in a refusal to accept one's insignificance.

516. Alexander did not weep because he could find no more lands to conquer. He wept because even great men are beset by imagination.

517. We see ourselves as protagonists in a poorly written script, surrounded by incompetent extras and maliciously placed props.

518. Vanity builds up kingdoms, but only so that the vain may observe their own vanity writ large.

519. It is not clear whether athletics more often improves health or shatters it. Why must sport be so fraught with danger and injury? Can it be that this is the real attraction?

520. Capitalism rewards narcissism and self-aggrandizement, and (let us be honest) this is what we love about it.

521. History repeats because those who make history cannot imagine persons other than themselves and their ilk manipulating the levers of power.

522. Art appeals to our pretensions. We wish to understand its subtleties so that we can claim to have done so.

523. No one is as self-deceived as are the utterly self-absorbed. None of us warrants such an intensity of concern.

524. No one is so irritating as those who remind us of ourselves when we were less than fully formed. We hate the sight of our former selves.

525. A broken man ceases to be concerned about the manner in which he is perceived. The broken man sees the folly of all such preoccupations.

526. Cowardice masquerades as disinterest.

527. Consumerism is idiocy gone to town in expensive regalia.

528. The bohemian is either the most courageous or the most cowardly of men—and cares not which.

529. Self-deprecation always cloaks arrogance. The truly humble do not speak of themselves at all.

530. A flatterer tells us what we want to hear. A skilled flatterer makes us want to hear what he has to tell.

531. Never attempt to impress anyone. The very impulse to do so betrays a position of weakness and subordination. What does it say about oneself that validation is sought in the judgment of the other?

532. Fame beckons to those who can experience joy only insofar as they feel themselves being watched. To be so dependent upon the public eye is to tether one's contentment to a whirlwind.

533. Ego is a tantalizing poison. It is a narcotic that one need not purchase, as it is always available wherever one finds oneself.

534. We secretly admire the huckster and charlatan because they prove that it is possible to be more highly regarded than one

deserves. Do any of us not aspire to seem better than we actually are?

535. The only sensible career goal is to be paid more than one deserves. All else is vanity.

536. Certainty is the greatest hubris.

537. If the matter is handled properly, there is at least as much advantage to be gained from being regarded as an imbecile as there is to be derived from being thought a genius.

538. Only a fool or a genius does not, at some point or other, believe himself to be a fraud.

539. No one attempts to assassinate the King's horse.

540. Nothing compels us to compete in those arenas in which we are vulnerable to defeat. Furthermore, nothing compels us to care about defeat, competition, or vulnerability.

541. It is unwise to trust anyone who thinks more highly of you than you truly deserve. It is, therefore, generally unwise to adhere too closely to a mother's counsel. Few mere mortals are what their mothers make them out to be.

542. The King and the deuce are equally valuable when building a house of cards.

543. We would be much less impressed with any work of art if we were to see it emerging gradually through every stage of production.

544. It is possible to be paralyzed by the fear of failure even when no great matter is at stake. The problem is not that one might

fail at this or that endeavor, but simply that one might fail at all. Why should failure, as common as it is, still induce such horror for so many?

545. Though we typically learn more from our failures than our successes, we still prefer success. What does this indicate about our commitment to learning?

546. Is it better to emulate great men, or to attempt to surpass them? Truly great men hope to be surpassed.

547. Most would prefer to be sure of themselves though they are dead wrong. Few can accept that we all fumble uncertainly along—hopefully blundering now and again into the light.

548. Man is an absurd ape who imagines that he is nature's *sine qua non*.

549. How is it possible that so many people fail to recognize that they are not nearly as fascinating to others as they are to themselves?

550. Animals do not kill each other over an abstraction, but only for vital (or, at least, visceral) purposes. Only man kills because of wounded honor. Man is the aggrieved animal.

551. The sweetest success is effortless and unsung.

552. It is only the mundane and the middling that allow for transcendence.

553. We manufacture excuses in much the same way that birds manufacture nests—and both offer comfort commensurate with our respective efforts.

554. Another's arrogance confronts us with the possibility of our own inferiority. This is why false pride is both ridiculous and irritating.

555. The transgression is always compounded and exacerbated by our attempt to hide it from the world.

556. Is a talent wasted simply because it is not placed on display for the approbation of crowds? Too often, we assume that skill kept to oneself is, therefore, frittered away. There are abilities that do not lend themselves to public consumption.

557. Fame is a sucker's bet. The payoff, rare as it is, does not warrant the wager.

558. The overvaluing of celebrity is almost a conspiracy. It can occur only with the complicity of the many and the megalomania of the few. The masses voluntarily participate in their own relative devaluation—and they buy tickets to the show.

559. Men build skyscrapers for the vanity of the penthouse.

Desire

560. Desire for something *else* is a tacit rejection of everything that stares us in the face. What is wrong with *this* that we must chase after something else?

561. Imagine having everything you ever wanted. Now what?

562. Desire and the object of desire are not exactly separate entities—or even separable. Can there be desire without object or direction? The effort to gain control of the objects of desire is also (or at least should be also) an effort to gain a degree of self-mastery. One may learn to attain one's goal, thereby altering the self in the acquisition, or one may learn how not to want the object any longer. This second type of alteration is not much in vogue, but it provides far greater, longer lasting, and reliable benefit.

563. Explanations of our desires and aversions are always fabrications and charades. None of us knows why we want the things that we do. Reason can offer no defense when desire stands trial.

564. Only a child can be authentically disappointed. The rest of us really ought to know better.

565. In a reasonable world, diamonds would be regarded as nothing more than nuggets of a relatively useless mineral. Desire for

them would be listed among psychological afflictions, and their display would be subject to bemusement—if not ridicule.

566. The wish to be admired by those for whom one feels contempt constitutes a compound perversion.

567. To desire power over others is to prove that one cannot be trusted to govern oneself.

568. We do not need help to quit our bad habits. We only need help to *want* to quit them.

569. Desire is the fountainhead of all misery, and we are drenched from the inside out. Almost every waking moment is besotted with grasping, clinging, and half-recognized lust for trifling ephemera. It is a strange wetness that burns.

570. We persist in activities that bore us to tears because we prefer familiarity to a challenge.

571. Pleasure is far more corrosive over the long run than pain. Libertines do not last—nor would they have it otherwise.

Work

572. Many people work long, arduous hours because they are desperate to avoid meeting up with themselves ... alone, without diversion. To be alone with one's thoughts is among the greatest unspoken horrors of the modern age.

573. It should be noted that, according to Genesis, work was a punishment levied against Adam for his disobedience. The rise of work coincides, biblically, with the fall from grace and the collapse of Eden. Perhaps a revaluation of the Judeo-Christian understanding of good and evil is in order for those who value leisure.

574. Responsibility is another form of slavery.

575. A career keeps us busy until we drop dead. For some, it also renders death more palatable and makes for a more seamless transition.

576. To labor at an occupation for which one feels contempt is to spend one's life contemptibly by one's own lights. It is a kind of psychic self-immolation to toil away, day after day, at efforts one regards as a waste of the limited vital energy with which one finds oneself endowed. To be treated as a mere means by another is to be ill used, but to voluntarily embrace such treatment is to prove it justified—and oneself worthy of no better.

577. Labor is the last resort of the unimaginative.

578. Why are we proud of the hours spent at work and ashamed of having overmuch leisure time? Should it not be the reverse?

579. There is no such thing as wasted time. Time does not lie in wait of employment.

580. Blunt instruments are, by nature, imprecise—but oh the satisfaction to be derived from the bludgeoning!

581. To display unfinished work is bad taste. It is like serving one's dinner guests a bloody roast straight from the slaughterhouse.

582. When one does more than one thing at a time, one does not exactly *do* any of the things that thereby get done. Things just sort of happen with oneself in the vicinity.

583. A pension is very similar to the money one leaves behind after a prostitute has served her purpose.

584. Misery in one's career virtually assures misery in one's retirement. A miserable retirement conduces to a welcoming embrace of death.

585. A career into which one does not stumble blindly is, at best, a bit of conscription.

Philosophy

586. Show me a philosopher with a theory and I'll show you a philosopher with a problem.

587. Is it the philosopher's job to conjure blind alleys? Perhaps.

588. Socrates declared the "unexamined life" not worth living. It is crucial to note that his examinations required what we, today, would describe as leisure. Had Socrates been burdened with the constraints of an occupation, as we moderns understand the concept, he would probably never have been tried and executed—and what a shame that would have been.

589. Skepticism is not exactly a theory—it is simply a refusal to ignore our limitations.

590. The philosopher is useful precisely to the extent that he destroys "philosophies".

591. Derrida's career was a put-on. The joke is that so many "intellectuals" failed to perceive this.

592. No child today grows up hoping to become a philosopher. Perhaps this is progress.

593. Nietzsche declared that anything that did not kill him outright made him stronger. He did not, one supposes, reckon on syphilis.

594. One cannot help but suspect a man who is offered power but refuses. Such a man must be a scoundrel, a fool, or a philosopher.

595. The sort of ignorance that we find in Plato's Socrates is a brand of ignorance worth cultivating. Would that we could all know as little as Socrates.

596. No one cares what philosophers have to say because philosophers long ago ceased saying anything about which it is possible for real people to care.

597. Some people have the capacity to know things without believing them. No one, however, may *know* a thing that is not actually worthy of belief.

598. Diogenes took up his lamp in search of an honest man. Today, we cannot even be bothered to seek another Diogenes. Honesty is not so much as held up as an ideal any longer, and only children actually expect it—mostly from their imaginary friends.

599. The charge of arbitrariness is itself quite frequently arbitrary. There are many contexts in which a principled defensibility is simply beside the point.

600. Ridicule is often the most effective refutation. One cannot offer a sincere objection where an opponent's position does not warrant serious consideration.

601. Do not engage an imbecile in debate—one can only be diminished in the enterprise.

602. There is no evidence to suggest that the best among us today have surpassed the ancient sages in understanding the human condition. The *Tao Te Ching* is not less revelatory than the mapping of the human genome.

603. Little has been learned that did not proceed ultimately from some guess or other.

604. Epictetus was, at one time, another man's property, but the Stoic sage was never as enslaved as is the average corporate executive today.

605. Once the point has been made, further argument is the equivalent of laying a chokehold on an unconscious opponent. It is both too much and of no avail.

606. If the tension is not exquisite, the arrow's flight is not true.

607. In Tibet, the concept of self-loathing was, until recently, unknown—an admirable ignorance.

608. Socrates mastered the marketplace by noting that it offered nothing he wanted. Virtue, he realized, was not for sale.

609. He who cannot enjoy frivolity is a malformed and pitiful being. He who cannot enjoy life without frivolity is a sage to be admired and emulated.

610. Is it possible to stumble blindly into enlightenment? If not, I hereby renounce all hope of it. That into which I cannot stumble has never been mine for the taking.

611. Why have sages such as Socrates, Buddha, and Jesus declined to write anything down? Was it wisdom that forestalled the writing? Perhaps the most important lessons are ineffable.

Then again, maybe they refrained from writing for lack of a worthy audience.

Death

612. We have good reasons to believe that bodies die. We have no evidence that persons die. Persons may or may not be bodies. Then again, persons may or may not actually exist. Bodies, on the other hand, are quite clearly real. In this respect, bodies deserve our trust more than persons.

613. Nearly everyone lives as if life does not end in death. Perhaps they are correct.

614. If we are mere bodies, then death is insignificant. If we are not mere bodies, then death reveals a practical joke.

615. Are we to believe that the soul leaves the body upon death? How so? Is it not the body that decays and disintegrates? The body leaves the stage. Where has a non-physical soul got to "go"?

616. Anyone who fears death clearly overestimates himself. Anyone who wishes for immortality clearly overestimates the human race.

617. The problem is not that so many men shall die realizing that they have not truly lived, but that so many men live as if they will not truly die. They lay up possessions as if to make them into a raft with which they may cross the Styx.

618. Each of us finds himself embedded within a story without beginning. Each of our stories, however, converges on the same ending.

619. We do not stand on the shoulders of giants. We clamber about on heaps of carcasses—denying to ourselves that we are destined to become part of the landscape.

620. Nothing is so secure as the grave.

621. There is all the difference in the world between a soldier and a warrior—but not nearly so much difference between their corpses.

622. Nature demands nothing of us other than death—and this, really, is not so much to ask.

623. If death is truly the end of us, then what is it that thereby comes to its end?

624. If we are immortal beings, then our suffering in this lifetime is insignificant. If we are *not* immortal beings, then our suffering in this lifetime is insignificant.

625. Lives may be wasted in the sense that death comes too early, but they may also be wasted in the sense that death comes not soon enough.

626. Lives end, but they do not cease to be. We simply lose sight of them.

627. When it comes to peace and quiet, nothing matches death.

628. For those who fear death, the best insurance is to avoid birth.

629. One cannot quite be an adult while both of one's parents are still alive. For this reason, at least, it is wise to wish one's parents long life.

630. It may be true that "all's well that ends well," but, for each of us, all ends in death.

631. No one can deprive us of death. This is the final freedom, and no good comes from postponing its realization when death is welcomed.

632. Some of us are not made for the world. We are not even fit for passing through.

633. Most of us find it difficult to imagine ourselves not existing after bodily death. This is peculiar given that most of us have no memory of existing before our parents met.

634. A graveyard is a silly thing. It is difficult to think of a more pointless waste of land and sculpted stone.

635. Laugh *first*. Do not assume that there will be an opportunity to laugh last.

636. The last few years are seldom worth the living—or so, at least, it appears from a safe distance.

637. There are works that do not exactly end—they simply stop somewhere.

Acknowledgments

A number of friends and colleagues have, in one way or another, contributed to this collection. Rachael Bennett, Tim McGarvey, Meghan Dupree, and Michelle Bushore all provided especially valuable criticism and feedback concerning earlier drafts. None of them should, for that reason, be held responsible for any inadequacies within the work. Those are all mine.

Others, far too numerous to mention, have unwittingly contributed in one form or another. They are all equally blameworthy.

978-0-595-45092-3
0-595-45092-X

Printed in the United States
97763LV00001B/52/A